Oils & Vinegars

A Gourmet's Guide

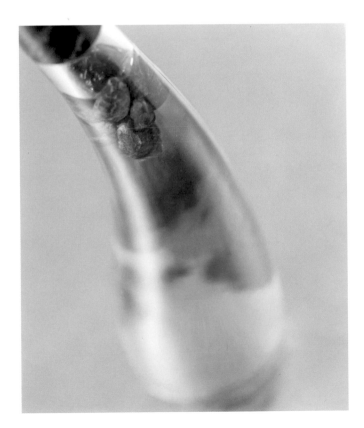

THIS IS A CARLTON BOOK

Text and Design © Carlton Books Limited, 1999

This edition published by Carlton Books Limited, 1999

A CIP catalogue record for this book is available from the
British Library

ISBN 1 85868 711 X

Project Editor: Camilla MacWhannell
Project art direction: Zoë Mercer, Diane Spender
Design and Editorial: Iain MacGregor, Neil Williams and Ian Chubb
Production: Alexia Turner
Picture Research: Loma Ainger
Special Photography: Howard Shooter

Printed and bound in Dubai

With special thanks to Tony from Lina Stores Ltd.,
Brewer Street, London.

PICTURE ACKNOWLEDGEMENTS

The publishers would like to thank the following sources for their
kind permission to reproduce the pictures in this book:
AKG London 20/Erich Lessing 10, 11, Van Gogh *The Olive Gatherers,
December 1889 Saint Remy* 35
Cephas/Mike Herringshaw 65b, Herbert Lehmann 85, Joris Luyten 51,
Alain Proust 29l, James Sparshatt 26, Stockfood 8-9, 33, 78,
TOP/Michel Barberousse 84, 93, TOP/Christine Fleurent 82t,
TOP/Pierre Hussenot 52, TOP/Peter Lippmann 89
et archive 14
Garden Picture Library 19/Guy Bouchet 34, Rex Butcher 63t, Phil
Jude 13, Tim Macmillan 65t, John Miller 19
Robert Harding Picture Library 69/Schuster 24
Image Select/Chris Fairclough 15
Frank Lane Picture Agency/JC Allen 39, B. Borrell 45, E & D Hosking
43, Jolyot/Sunset 62, 63b, Mark Newman 42, Chris Newton 66, Keith
Rushforth 74, Winifried Wisniewski 16, Martin Withers 40
Panos Pictures/Pietro Cenini 50
Tony Stone Images 25/Thierry Borredon 21, Michael Busselle 4, Joe
Cornish 25, Ian O'Leary 5, 59, Steve Outram 22
Science Photo Libray/John Bavosi 29tr, R.Maisonneuve, Publiphoto
Diffusion 91, Alfred Pasieka 28
Howard Shooter 1, 2, 6-7, 23, 30, 31, 36, 41, 44, 46, 48, 53-55, 60,
64, 67, 70-72, 76, 77, 80, 81, 82b, 83, 87, 92
Marco Verona 12, 17

Every effort has been made to acknowledge correctly and contact the
source and/copyright holder of each picture, and Carlton Books
Limited apologises for any unintentional errors or omissions which
will be corrected in future editions of this book.

Oils & Vinegars

A Gourmet's Guide

KAREN FARRINGTON

CARLTON

CONTENTS

INTRODUCTION

Oils and vinegars were once considered utilitarian and warranted little attention. A buyer was likely to be guided by purse rather than palate since the stock available was extremely bland and limited. All that has changed with the vogue for Mediterranean cuisine. Simple and delicious, it relies almost entirely on olive oil for its beneficial unsaturated fat content and is consequently very healthy to incorporate in your diet. Hot on its heels, balsamic vinegar has become the latest kitchen trend. The more people learned about olive oil and balsamic vinegar the more they wanted to know. It has led to consumers taking a fresh view of a whole range of different oils and vinegars. Meals now have new depth – but there's a price penalty. As with every commodity it is best to know exactly what you are buying, and for what purpose, before splashing out.

OLIVE OIL

To the Ancient Greeks, the olive tree was a gift of the gods. According to Homer, who lived in the eighth century BC, it gave us 'liquid gold'. Three centuries later the Greek dramatist Sophocles (ca. 496–406 BC) lauded it as 'the tree that stands unequalled'. For many it yields the fundamental ingredient of their daily diet. They are the lucky ones, for recent research has indicated that olive oil is something of a prevention or even cure for today's plagues of heart disease and cancer.

The Story of Olives

According to mythology the goddess Pallas Athena made a gift of the olive tree to the ancient Greeks. The story goes that she and Poseidon, god of the sea, were competing for the protection of Attica, an honour granted to whoever offered the gift of greatest value. Poseidon chose a horse while Athena sprouted the olive tree 'capable of giving a flame for lighting up the night; of soothing wounds; of being a precious food, both rich in flavour and a source of energy'.

RIGHT: THE GODDESS ATHENA, BY GREEK SCULPTOR MYRON.

BELOW: NOAH'S ARK – A CATALAN MANUSCRIPT ILLUMINATION.

The olive tree was deemed by the Greek people to be of great worth. In gratitude the people named their primary city Athens in honour of the goddess. The story of her gift is related in a tableau on the side of the Parthenon.

Pallas Athena was, according to legend, born from the head of Zeus, and became the favourite child of the deity. Paradoxically she was the Greek goddess of both war and wisdom and the Parthenon was the centre of worship to her. She caused an olive tree to grow at the gates of the Acropolis, and Greek gods were thought to have been born under the branches of the olive tree.

When the Athenians returned from their Median wars their city was in ruins, but the sacred olive tree was still there, having prevailed over the destruction.

For centuries the olive has been a symbol of peace, friendship and fertility. In the Bible, a dove returned to Noah's ark with an olive branch to prove that the floods had subsided. Historically a crown of olives was used to decorate a victor in sports competitions. Indeed, the first Olympic flame was carried on an olive branch and athletes of the era were coated with olive oil.

The Bible includes nearly 100 references to olive trees and a further 140 to olive oil. The Qur'an, too, has a place for the olive tree 'that sprouts on Mount Sinai and provides oil as a condiment to the table'. Muslims believe it to be 'the Blessed Tree, neither of the East nor the West'.

The Egyptians grew their own olives for the table but imported Syrian olive oil. Mummies have been found with olive branches around them and sometimes olive oil was used in the embalming process. According to the Romans, Hercules walked along the shores of the Mediterranean clutching his olive staff. Every time it struck the ground an olive tree took root there.

This was the noble heritage of the olive in the Mediterranean and the Middle East, but it took a long time for it to reach Europe. Just 20 years ago olive oil could only be obtained in England in small bottles from chemists' shops and its flavour was nothing to compare with that of freshly made olive oil, nor its colour and aroma. Advances in transport have made it possible for higher quality olive oil to reach distant markets quickly, and this has led to a boom in popularity.

Olive Oil Production

Olive oil is squeezed from the fruit of the evergreen olive tree (*Olea europea*), of which there are some 700 different varieties existing. Olive trees are thought to have originated in Asia Minor where cultivation is believed to have begun some 7000 years ago. From there the trees spread around the Mediterranean and have come to characterise the region. Olives are grown to eat, to make cooking oil or to make a tasty condiment. On average each tree produces between 33 and 44 pounds of olives, which in turn makes between three to four litres of oil.

O lives are picked in the winter months between November and March, six to eight months after their small greenish white flowers have sprouted.

The olives contain no oil until they are pastel green in colour. That's when a chemical reaction changes sugars and acids into oil. The later the fruit is harvested the greater their content of oil. However, overly ripe olives contain more acidity than those gathered when they are still immature, and this will taint the oil. Only experience can tell the olive grower what to harvest, and when, for optimum results.

RIGHT: AN OLIVE ORCHARD IN ANATOLIA, TURKEY.

BELOW: OLIVES CONTAIN OIL AFTER CHANGING FROM GREEN TO BLACK.

The first problem facing olive-growers is harvesting. For thousands of years this has been a painstaking task undertaken by hand. A refinement on the method was to prop a ladder between the branches and stand aloft, dragging through the foliage with giant wooden combs. Although this still goes on there are mechanical 'branch-shakers' available now to farmers which will deposit the fruit into nets strung below the trees. This way the olives are saved from being damaged by falling to the ground – very important since bruised and dirty fruit is most likely to yield rancid oil. Even with branch or trunk shakers the final picking to clear the tree of its fruit is done by hand. It is the labour intensive picking process where half the costs of olive oil manufacture are incurred.

In short, leaves and branches are discarded before the olives are weighed, then thoroughly washed at the mill or frantoio. In hot climates this all happens within 24 hours of them being picked. Olives picked in cooler areas may benefit from standing for a day or two, allowing them to be warmed by the sun so they will give greater amounts of oil. But olives destined for oil production are kept no longer than three days. Left on their own for too long the olives will begin to ferment and deterioration of this kind in the crop will affect the quality of the oil. Olives are, of course, pressed whole with skins and stones.

The Process

The first step in oil production is to grind the olives into a pulp. Once this was done with granite millstones but today easy-clean stainless steel apparatus has taken precedence. This process extracts the first pressing. It is important that this is done without intense heat, which would increase the quantity of oil but in so doing would harm its quality.

Hence the much-vaunted phrase 'cold-pressed', which is often used in relation to olive oil. Cold pressing is believed to keep olive oil's nutritional qualities intact but means that it has a shorter shelf life than its heat-treated rivals. However, heat is generally used in secondary pressings to extract the maximum amount of oil. The dark brown paste is then spread onto woven mats — once made of hemp, now of polypropylene — which are stacked on a central pole and submitted to hydraulic presses, as many as 40 at a time. In this way the paste offers the least resistance to the power of the press. Oil seeps through the mats and into a collection tank at the bottom. It's not just oil coming out, of course — there's water and some vegetable matter too. Once the pressed liquid was left to settle and the oil and water naturally separated so the oil could be siphoned off. Oil bottled after this procedure might bear the title 'Afficrato'. Today it is more usual to find a rapidly rotating machine which takes one from the other by means of centrifugal force.

Even then there may still be oil left in the residue. It is shipped to a refinery so that the last drop may be extracted, and the vegetable waste is used as animal feed or fertiliser.

Modern technology has given olive growers another alternative which is pressure-free. This is a system in which the olive paste is spread over countless numbers of rotating stainless steel blades. In the act of cutting into the olive pulp the oil is released and descends down the blades into a collection point. The system, which works by taking advantage of the difference in surface tension between oil and water, produces a pure product.

Olive farmers may work independently or be part of a co-operative scheme. If a farmer is in charge of the olives from blossom to bottle then he is known as a single-estate producer. More usually a farmer will dispatch his crop to a central point, one of many to contribute to an industrial-sized batch.

LEFT: GIANT STONES WERE ONCE USED TO PULP THE OLIVES.

BELOW: AN OLIVE PRESS.

Blends and Varieties

The end product may range from excellent through indifferent to downright bad. Those oils judged sub-standard, or too acidic, will be blended with quality oil to improve them.

DIFFERENT TYPES OF OLIVE TREE MAY BE GROWN TOGETHER IN THE SAME FIELD.

Although some olive oils are blended, that does not necessarily demean the product. Even the most sought after oils may well be a blend. After all, a grower may have one, two or more different types of olive trees in his grove, a 'field blend'. By virtue of the initial pressing of different types of olives a blend is instantly created.

The bigger corporations which produce olive oils use oils not only from different farms but from different countries. It is often impossible to distinguish just where

the olives have come from by looking at the label. For instance, an oil which appears to hail from Italy may contain considerable quantities of imported Spanish oil. At the moment there's no law which says derivative sources have to be identified to the consumer. However, in 1996 the European Union established a labelling system known as DOC (Denominaçiones de Origen or, in France, Appellation d'Origine Controlée), and top grade olive oils often bear such a label.

In the end it is the taste that counts, and that's often a case of personal preference. Suppliers have responded to different tastes around the globe with a whole range of products. The most distinctively flavoursome remain in the Mediterranean where the national palates are appreciative of strong-tasting oil. In Britain the trend for using olive oil is still relatively new and therefore blander lines stock the shelves. In

America the big producers have had success with 'light' olive oil in which much of the flavour is removed.

Olive oil on the grocer's shelf often comes in different grades. Extra virgin oils are the best quality with the most pleasant bouquet and the finest flavour with the least acidity. The chemical measurement which defines extra virgin is the content of oleic acid. It consists of only one gram of oleic acid to every 100 grams of oil. Extra virgin oil is best used cold, in salad dressings or on previously cooked pasta to savour its flavour. Save on expense by never using it for cooking – a cheaper alternative will do this job just as well.

The next rung down is virgin olive oil which may have up to but no more than two grams of oleic acid per hundred grams of oil. Still, its taste and aroma remain superior to olive oil.

Those bottles designated 'olive oil' almost certainly contain oil with a higher acid content that has then been blended with virgin olive oil for general kitchen use including roasting. Despite the presence of virgin oil in the blend it is known simply as olive oil. Its acidity will probably be low but that is as a result of chemical refinement rather than cold pressing.

Beyond olive oil comes olive pomace oil, a refined oil squeezed out at the end of the oil-making procedure. Virgin oil is added but it doesn't make the grade as olive oil and a distinction should be made on the label. This is the lowest quality of olive oil approved for human consumption. Crude olive-pomace oil and lampanate virgin olive oil are generally for refining or technical purposes rather than consumption.

EVEN THE BEST OLIVE OILS MAY BE A BLEND.

Properties and Storage

An elegant bottle of olive oil evokes sun-drenched groves clinging to bleached hillsides which softly rise and fall beneath an endless blue sky. The delectable aroma and piquant flavour of olive oil seems almost elemental, its ability to feed, heal and sooth being legendary.

When olive oil is cloudy it is almost certainly cold. The oleic acid in it has a tendency to coagulate in chilly conditions. Olive oil should never be stored in the refrigerator but should be tightly sealed and kept away from heat or light. When cloudy oil is brought back to room temperature the clarity should return. Some people choose to store olive oil in a green glass wine bottle to protect it from the ultraviolet rays in sunshine.

Olive oil can be stored in glass, stainless steel or ceramic containers.

Plastic is less popular in case the oil absorbs some of the compounds used in the manufacture of the bottle. Olive oil has a sponge-like ability to take on other flavours which is why it must be stored in isolation.

It will keep for a year, but consumers are ill-advised to keep it for much longer. Pliny the Elder (23–79 AD) made observations in his lifetime which still hold good today: 'Age imparts an unpleasant taste to oil, which is not the case with wine, and after a year it is old. Nature shows forethought in this, if one chooses to interpret it this way, since it is not necessary to use up wine which is produced for getting merry; indeed, the pleasant overripeness that comes with maturity encourages us to keep it. She did not, however, wish us to be niggardly with oil, and has made its use widespread, even among the masses, because of the need to use it up quickly.'

An estimated seven million families are involved in the cultivation of 850 million olive trees around the world, in countries as far flung as China and Chile, Australia, Afghanistan and Angola. Traditionally the olive grower has an enduring, homely image with lines on his weather-beaten face to match the grooves of an old olive bough. Yet the business of olives and oils has a turnover of many millions of dollars a year.

KEEP OLIVE OIL IN A COOL, DARK PLACE. IF IT GOES CLOUDY RETURN THE BOTTLE TO ROOM TEMPERATURE.

National Industries

To some countries the growing of olives and subsequent production of oil is economically vital.

Spain

Olives first came to Spain on the ships of the Phoenicians, those outstanding navigators and traders who came from North Africa and the Middle East. The Greeks also travelled there bearing olive treasure. Today Spain produces more olive oil than any other nation.

Occupying Romans further developed the production of olive oil with the introduction of a screw press. Their excellent lines of communication helped improve distribution, too. We can surmise that olive groves in Spain were notably bountiful as the world's oldest cookery book, 'Reconquindaria', by Apicius makes many references to olive oil from Spain.

Later still Spain fell into the hands of the Moors who likewise capitalised on the abundant growth of olives under warm Spanish skies. Indeed, the Spanish word for oil is 'aceite', derived directly from the Arab word 'al-zait', meaning olive juice.

It was the Spanish conquistadors who took olives to the new world. The climate of California is as suitable as that of Spain and olive trees began to thrive there under the watchful gaze of the Franciscan friars. Likewise the olive travelled to parts of Latin America along with the Catholic faith. That's why olives grow in Mexico, Peru, Chile and Argentina, where one of the original plants from Europe, the Arauco olive, still grows some 400 years after its introduction.

There are an estimated 215 million olive trees in Spain, covering two million hectares of the country's agricultural land. Eighty percent of Spanish olive oil production takes place in Andalusia, in particular the regions of Jaén and Cordoba. The annual production amounts to about 600,000 metric tonnes per year, about a third of which is exported. Olive oil from Spain is sold in over 95 countries.

One of the key national dishes in Spain is tapas, a variety of appetiser from Andalusia, each one containing copious quantities of olive oil. The Spanish like to fry almonds with paprika and will use the entire contents of a small bottle of olive oil to fry eight oz (225g) of nuts. Then there's Spanish tortilla, better known in some parts of the world as omelette, in which the potatoes are fried in half a pint of olive oil. Generosity with olive oil is bred into the Spanish spirit.

RIGHT: SPANISH CONQUISTADORS TOOK OLIVE OIL TO THE NEW WORLD.

FAR RIGHT: OLIVE GROVES ARE TYPICAL OF THE ANDALUSIAN COUNTRYSIDE.

Greece

Today Greece is the third largest producer of olive oil in the world – there are 11 million olive trees on the island of Crete alone and an estimated 137 million trees nationwide, some over 1,000 years old. Of the 300,000 tons of olive oil produced in Greece each year, about 70 percent of it is classed as extra virgin. Greece is also the biggest consumer of olive oil per head of population. On average, every man, woman and child consumes five gallons a year.

Somehow Greece has acquired the image of producing inferior oil to the rest of Europe. There's no basis for this. Bear in mind that Greece exports much of its finest home-grown oil to Italy, and the Italians are very fussy about olive oil quality. If the Greeks are

BELOW: A WHITEWASHED CHURCH NESTLING IN GROVES WHICH GROW IN THE FOOTHILLS OF THE GREEK MOUNTAINS.

trailing the rest of the Mediterranean it is not in the quality of their oil but in their marketing strategies.

The most famous olive grown by the Greeks is the Kalamata, from the region of the same name, which is both converted to oil and used at the table. Koroneiki olives are also a popular choice. Helena Hurst, a former teacher at the Cordon Bleu cookery school in London, had a Greek father who used olive oil 'in

everything'. Her concern today is that few people know how fresh olive oil tastes: 'The flavour of fresh cold pressed olive oil is just incredible. It is nothing compared to what you get elsewhere. The problem is that you never know what goes into a bottle bought here unless you pay big money for it.'

To recreate a flavour of Greece here in northern Europe she marinates olives at home using tinned fruit. After draining off the brine she mixes the olives with crushed garlic, lemon rind, oregano, pepper and olive oil. This is then left for five days to marinate. The olives will keep for up to three months in the fridge.

ABOVE: TABLE OLIVES ARE SOAKED IN OIL TO DISPEL THE NATURALLY BITTER FLAVOUR.

Italy

Most years Italy is the second largest producer of olives in the world (only a climatic disaster like a drought or prolonged frost is likely to topple Spain as the world's leading producer). However, Italy remains a top importer of olive oil too. They use foreign products to blend with their own home-produced oils.

The Romans were enthusiastic promulgators of the olive and fairly covered the boot of Italy with groves. Only the region of Val d'Aosta in the north-west of the country is devoid of olive trees.

After the collapse of the Roman empire the olive industry went into decline. But it was saved from obscurity by its versatility, and later assumed great importance by providing fuel for the lamps in Catholic churches.

Monks established olive groves in Apulia, the heel of Italy's boot, in the 13th century. Specially designed flat bottomed boats were built in Venice to ferry jars of olive oil from the productive south to parts of cooler northern Italy.

Olive oil from Tuscany remains perhaps the most famous of the Italian varieties. Olives grown in the region are predominantly the high-yielding Frantoio, the equally productive Moraiolo and the disease-resistant Leccino. While the region produces more extra virgin oil than any other it still only provides a fraction of the country's output.

America

Olive groves established by Franciscan monks from Spain enabled America to produce its own oil. Business thrived until the end of the 19th century when imports began to undercut the price of the home-produced oil and improvements in canning persuaded farmers to favour table olives instead. However, olive oil production in California is getting underway again in earnest, spurred on by its proven health benefits. It looks set to mimic the success of the region's wine makers.

France

France is a minnow in the sea of olive oil producers but the oil it produces is of excellent quality. The centres of production are in Provence and extend around the Mediterranean coast.

It is an important constituent of the Gallic diet and perhaps the best tribute to it was paid by Mme Jeanne Calment, of Arles, on her 121st birthday. She confessed that she ate olive oil at every meal and rubbed it into her skin daily. 'I have only one wrinkle – and I am sitting on it', she declared.

RIGHT: FRENCH OLIVE PRODUCTION IS CENTRED IN PROVENCE.

BELOW: TUSCANY IS FAMOUS FOR ITS OLIVES BUT THE REST OF ITALY PRODUCES FINE OIL TOO.

Healthy Alternative

Olive oil is credited with many beneficial qualities. Its most celebrated attribute is its ability to help prevent one of the twentieth century's biggest killers, coronary heart disease.

Research in Europe and America has revealed that western and northern European diets rich in saturated fatty acids increase the incidence of coronary heart disease. Not surprisingly, there is a lower risk of heart disease for those in Mediterranean areas enjoying a diet weighed with monounsaturated fatty acids. Spain, the biggest producer of olive oil, enjoys one of the lowest rates of heart disease in the western world. This is why a majority of health professionals agree that a Mediterranean-style diet in which olive oil is the principle source of fat is so meritorious.

The foundation of the 'eat Mediterranean' diet theory was the Seven Countries study which began back in 1958. Its purpose was to study the health risks confronting middle aged men, and included diet, exercise and smoking. The Finns had the highest mortality rates, followed by the Americans, while the Japanese, Greeks and Italians scored lowest in the heart disease stakes. Historically the Japanese have included little fat in their diet so that result was predictable. Yet Greeks and Italians enjoyed a high fat diet with most of the fat coming in the form of olive oil. It was the first indication that olive oil was far healthier than other oils. To further prove the case the study went on to witness Mediterraneans forsaking a traditional diet in subsequent years in favour of a Western-style one, with its greater emphasis on red meat. As diet trends changed the rates of heart disease rose.

RESEARCH HAS PROVED THAT OLIVE OIL CAN HELP REDUCE THE RISK OF HEART DISEASE.

Does Olive Oil Benefit the Body?

It has a significant effect on cholesterol, a substance which is made in the liver and helps to form cells and blood.

A Mediterranean-style diet will help protect your body against
- heart disease
- a second heart attack
- diabetes
- obesity
- some cancers, such as breast and colon

It does so by
- lowering blood cholesterol
- lowering blood pressure
- controlling body weight
- preventing blood clots
- protecting the body against cancer-forming free radicals

Without going into the complex chemical formulae there are two types of cholesterol, one which is bad (Low Density Lipoprotein) and the other good (High Density Lipoprotein). LDLs fur up the arteries of the body by leaving deposits on the vessel walls. Arteries vary in size but none are enormously wide and some are very small indeed, just 2mm or a twelfth of an inch in diameter, making fat deposits a major problem.

So the cholesterol which sticks on artery walls constricts the blood flow and may ultimately lead to coronaries and strokes when vital organs are starved of blood and the oxygen it carries. Conversely the HDLs carry cholesterol away from the artery walls and tissues, returning it to the liver, where it was originally made, for excretion. It is believed that vitamin E present in olive oil acts as an antioxidant to break down the fatty streaks made by LDLs. Olive oil is, by the way, naturally cholesterol free.

Olive oil is high in monounsaturated fats (known as MUFAs) which help to reduce the bad cholesterol in the body without inhibiting the work of the good cholesterol – transporting fat around the body. Fat contains vitamins like A, D, E and K and is an even greater source of energy than carbohydrates and proteins. Through the consumption of olive oil a vital balance is achieved.

Mediterranean meals typically contain a lot of fruit and vegetables, many of which are eaten raw. There's plenty of starch in the form of bread, cereals, rice, couscous and pasta which provide energy and fibre and satisfy hunger. In addition there is fish, particularly oily fish, and lean meat. It is a diet rich in dairy products, like yoghurt and cheese. Alcohol, predominantly wine, is usually an accompaniment to meals.

For those who follow this kind of diet, the outlook is all good. It is attributed to a reduction in heart disease and the prevention of a second heart attack. It also offers protection against diabetes, obesity and some cancers, notably breast and colon cancer. Olive oil aids digestion and may help protect against gastric problems. It can also act as an efficient laxative. It assists the growth of bones by fighting the loss of calcium. Further, it is also thought to fight the effects of ageing on the functions of the brain.

Although science has yet to prove a conclusive case for olive oil in the battle against cancer it is widely believed that more than a third of cancer deaths can be attributed to dietary factors, and cancer mortality rates are generally highest in the northern and eastern European countries and lower in the Mediterranean countries. Also, the anti-carcinogenic effects of fruit and vegetables through the vitamins and minerals they contain is well established.

Of course, olive oil and the foods of sun-rich countries around the Mediterranean will not in isolation protect the body from all ills. It is important to take regular exercise, to keep a healthy body weight, to avoid smoking and reduce stress through relaxation.

RIGHT: THIS ARTERY HAS CLEARLY BECOME CLOGGED UP WITH FATTY DEPOSITS.

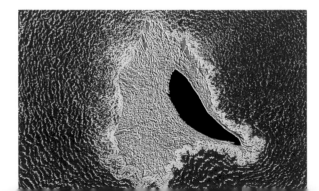

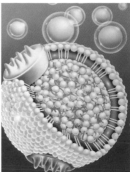

ABOVE:
'BAD' CHOLESTEROL –
A LOW DENSITY
LIPOPROTEIN.

LEFT: SEAFOOD CAN
FORM PART OF A
HEALTHY DIET.

Tasting Olive Oil

Each olive oil has its own distinct aroma and flavour, in much the same way that wine differs in region and vintage. The expert will indulge in a 'tasting' to establish the preferred variety, a journey of sensory delight.

1. Place the olive oil into a glass bowl and stand it against a white background in order to appreciate the colour. Its hue may be anything from straw yellow to bold green. Remember that colour is not, generally speaking, an indicator of quality. Unscrupulous producers have been known to meddle with natural colours by using olive tree leaves as an enhancement while an orange tint may possibly indicate the oil has been carelessly stored and is not at its best, but these are merely generalisations.

2. Swirl the oil around the bowl to maximise the aroma before inhaling deeply. Olive oil may be pungent, spicey, nutty, even chocolatey. Study its body, too. Its consistency should be uniform and fluid. Greasy-looking oils and thin, watery oils point to a sub-standard variety.

3. Use a teaspoon, plain bread or even a steamed vegetable for tasting and use the same method for each sample of oil to compare like with like. When it's in your mouth breathe air through it as if it were a wine. A fine oil will leave the mouth after making its initial impact. Poor oil lingers like axle grease.

4. Cleanse the palate with a glass of water and a piece of dry bread between each tasting. Oils which leave a fatty feeling around the mouth or an acidic aftertaste are to be avoided. Those with flavours which range from buttery, bland, fruity, peppery through to sweet are choice. In some the flavour of olives is paramount. In others there is merely a whisper of the original fruit. A strongly flavoured oil may be chosen above its lighter, sweeter competitor for one recipe while another dressing calls for entirely different qualities. Each olive-growing region has fostered its own character which is appropriate for the local cuisine. An expert may come to know the difference. A final choice of olive oil is made in consideration of the appearance, the taste and the price.

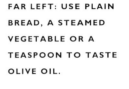

FAR LEFT: USE PLAIN BREAD, A STEAMED VEGETABLE OR A TEASPOON TO TASTE OLIVE OIL.

THE COLOUR OF OLIVE OIL CAN BE ENHANCED TO MAKE IT APPEAR A BETTER PRODUCT.

Include Olive Oil in Your Daily Diet

Dip bread into a saucer of extra virgin olive oil instead of using butter or margarine.

Toss hot or cold vegetables in a couple of tablespoons of olive oil, together with salt, freshly ground pepper and some lemon juice.

Thicken stock or broth with olive oil instead of butter or meat juices.

Roast cubed root vegetables including swede, carrot, parsnip and potatoes in olive oil with whole garlic cloves, salt, pepper and parsley.

Seal meat or poultry by brushing it with olive oil before baking.

Make croutons for soup by baking squares of sliced bread or chunks of French bread in olive oil until crisp.

Sauté bananas, apples, pears and other fruit in olive oil, sprinkle with sugar and cinnamon and serve as a sweet.

Sauté nuts in olive oil to bring out their full flavour.

Add a drop of olive oil to the pan when pasta is cooking.

Immediately it is drained toss pasta in olive oil to stop it sticking together.

Use olive oil in cake and cookie baking. Reduce the quantity of shortening in recipes by 25 percent when substituting olive oil.

Coat hands with olive oil when rolling and spreading pizza dough to stop it sticking.

Marinate olives at home. If fresh olives are not readily available, substitute tinned. Strain off the brine and immerse in olive oil with crushed garlic, lemon rind, oregano, salt and pepper.

Replace the shortening in carrot cake recipes with oil. It gives a dense texture which suits carrot cake, rather than an open texture which generally indicates the use of butter.

If olive oil is too expensive for your budget stretch it by mixing with cheaper sunflower oil. This will also suit anyone who dislikes an overwhelming taste of olive oil.

Grow an Olive Tree

We already know that olive oil is high in vitamin E and a good source of natural antioxidants. So it should be no surprise to learn that these two qualities are to be found in the raw olive, a hard button of a fruit most often found bobbing about in a Martini or decorating the table as an hors d'ouevre. It is enough to tempt the greenhouse gardener to give houseroom to an olive tree.

AN OLIVE TREE WILL OUTLIVE THE PERSON WHO PLANTED IT BY CENTURIES.

O live trees do not bear fruit until they are between five and eight years old. Only when they notch up 35 growing years will they be fully productive and harvests will occur every year for at least 150 years. Even at that great age the tree is far from spent. It will flower and fruit – albeit less prolifically – for centuries. Some experts believe there are trees in existence today which are more than 1,000 years old, and when an old tree dies it is not unusual for new shoots to sprout around its base.

So you can see it is less of a tree, more of a family heirloom that is grown!

It is best to grow an olive tree from a propagated cutting. The next consideration for a young olive tree is warmth. If the temperature dips below 10 degrees fahrenheit (-12 degrees centigrade) the growth is at best impaired, and at worst the tree will die altogether. However, a chill in winter which will bring the tree into a dormant state is an asset.

Olive trees appreciate a dry climate and can withstand comparatively high winds, at least until they are laden with fruit. The quality of the soil is not paramount. Like a fellow fruit of the Mediterranean, the grape, shallow-rooted olives will flourish on stony ground although pot-bound varieties would appreciate a rich mix to promote swift growth. Feed them on nitrogen and beware of watering around the root for fear of sparking crown rot. Those growing olives commercially will plant up to 200 trees per acre and, to be financially viable, must look to having at least five acres in production.

Olives are either green or black. In fact, black olives are simply ripened green fruits. As raw olives are bitter to eat they are marinated in oil, water or brine for between one and six months to remove the vile-tasting oleuropin from their skins.

A home-grown olive tree is unlikely to yield sufficient fruit to make olive oil, especially if cultivated in northerly climes. Nor is the fruit so desirable that any aspiring grower would blithely tackle the task of cultivation.

It is the silver green foliage that makes the olive tree so visually appealing, along with its gnarled trunk. The aesthetically pleasing appearance of the olive made it a subject for artists Van Gogh and Rembrandt. Indeed Van Gogh produced no fewer than 19 works featuring olive trees.

THE OLIVE GATHERERS, **BY VINCENT VAN GOGH.**

OTHER OILS

In addition to the olive there are other plants, seeds and crops from which oil can be extracted, with varying results. Choose a standard vegetable oil for deep frying where cost is as much a consideration as taste. But if the purse permits treat yourself to a walnut oil for salad dressings where just a little can be used to immense effect.

Safflower oil

Safflower oil is made from hardy safflowers, which are of the thistle family. These plants are ideally suited to arid areas as they can withstand long periods without water thanks to a sturdy tap root which will extend up to 12 feet to find a water source. This gives the safflower an advantage over crop competitors like soybean, corn and rape. Growers of safflowers in western America rotate it with wheat, barley and tomatoes. But these are much less of a spectacle. The safflowers grow to four feet in height and are topped with yellow, orange and gold blooms which will rival sunflowers for sheer splendour.

Safflowers are planted between late January and early May and the harvest is between four and eight months, when the thistle heads are dry and brown. The combine harvesters move in to mow the safflower fields, and seeds are separated and crushed for oil. The residue forms a high protein meal which is ideal for animal feed.

Such is its vivid colouring the plant is sometimes known as false saffron. High in monounsaturates and polyunsaturates but largely lacking in vitamins, it is an all-purpose cooking oil.

Sunflower oil

High in polyunsaturates and a good source of vitamin E, pale, delicately-flavoured sunflower oil can be used for almost everything. However, like soya oil it sometimes leaves sticky deposits during frying. Commercially it is often turned into spreads and dressings.

Sunflowers are grown in France, Spain, America, Russia and other eastern European countries where the rows of nodding blooms which turn to follow the sun create a memorable impression.

Extra virgin sunflower oil is now available. This is sunflower oil which has been cold pressed in the same way as olive oil, rather than refined. The flavour is light and nutty and thus rivals olive oil in its uses.

Corn oil

Also known as maize oil, it is often used for frying because it is a stable oil which in normal circumstances is unlikely to ignite. It is high in polyunsaturates and vitamins and, in addition to its use as a cooking oil, may be used in the pharmaceutical industry.

ABOVE: CORN OIL IS IDEAL FOR FRYING.

LEFT: SUNFLOWERS CAN BE REFINED OR COLD PRESSED TO PRODUCE OIL.

Cotton seed oil

As the name implies, this oil is derived from the seed of the cotton plant. Consequently, it is used primarily in cotton-growing areas as a cheap by-product of the fabric-making process. Its flavour is characteristic of Egyptian cuisine. Some cotton-seed oil finds its way into margarine and shop-bought fried products after being added to vegetable oil.

Rapeseed oil

A rape crop never goes unnoticed. The bright yellow flowers are eye-scalding and can be found lighting up fields in Canada, Britain, Europe and America. It was first introduced to northern Europe by the Romans who, in the absence of olive trees, exploited the crop for oil.

Its popularity has risen recently since being acclaimed as the oil with less saturated fat than any other. And after olive oil it is rapeseed oil which boasts the highest level of monounsaturated fatty acids, which can reduce the risk of heart disease. The flavour is bland so it sits well with other foods. It also remains one of the best value oils around.

Rapeseed oil is most frequently used in Canada, Japan, China and India where it has been largely re-christened canola oil. Another name for it is 'lear' oil which stands for 'low erucic acid rapeseed'. Sometimes it is mistakenly called mustard oil as the closely-related plants look similar. It can be used for frying, baking, spreads and dressings.

Sesame seed oil

There are two types of sesame seed oil, distinguishable by colour. The light oil is nutty and versatile, while the darker one is rich. Sesame seed oil is imbued with a distinctive taste and smell. Like olive oil, there's little processing in its production. Sesame seeds are simply roasted, crushed and filtered. Its cost is consequently high but the taste is strong and little is needed to make an impact. Those who find the flavour too intrusive may find a teaspoonful mixed with grapeseed oil sufficient.

Primarily it is used in oriental cookery. It is as well to put sesame seed oil in at the end of the cooking process rather than at the beginning because it is quick to burn.

RIGHT: SESAME SEED OIL BURNS AT A LOW TEMPERATURE, SO ADD IN THE FINAL MOMENTS OF COOKING.

BELOW: A VIVIDLY COLOURED RAPE CROP.

Pumpkin seed oil

A moody, dark oil, similar at first glance to soy sauce or balsamic vinegar, but with a powerful flavour. The home of pumpkin seed oil is Steiermark in Austria. It is useful for salad dressings, can be dripped on hot or cold vegetables and can also be splashed onto fish.

Grapeseed oil

This oil, extracted from grape pips, is linked to the major wine growing areas. That means the centres of manufacture are France, Italy and, to a lesser extent, America. The grape seeds are, of course, a by-product of the wine industry and that makes it an eco-friendly oil as no meadowland or pasture is sacrificed for its production.

In composition it is low in saturated fat, with half the amount that is in olive oil, and high in polyunsaturated fat. Long before scientific knowledge about the health benefits of oils existed, grapeseed oil was sold in French pharmacies as a remedy for high cholesterol levels.

It contains vitamin E, boasts a long shelf life and has about the highest flash point of all cooking oils. It is pale, delicate and quite neutral. It is nevertheless an agreeably tasting oil, for frying and general culinary use. Many people use it when making mayonnaise.

Avocado oil

Extracted from the inedible stone of the avocado, this is a neutral oil, almost colourless and fragrance-free. It has no discernible flavour and is used for culinary and cosmetic purposes. Avocadoes and olives are generally the only two fruits to be pressed for oil.

It has extremely high levels of beneficial monounsaturated fat in its constitution, exceeding that of almond and olive oil.

RIGHT: AVOCADO OIL IS SQUEEZED FROM THE STONE OF THE FRUIT.

BELOW: PUMPKINS CAN BE PRESSED TO PRODUCE A DARK, POTENT OIL.

Groundnut oil

Also known as peanut oil, it is clear in colour and usually mild to taste. Often peanut oil is used in Chinese cookery. For this purpose chefs may prefer the stronger tasting brands which can be found in oriental grocery shops. It can also be stored indefinitely without detriment to its quality. However, it is thought to cause a severe allergic reaction in a small minority of people.

Soya oil

Made from the bean, soya oil is an inexpensive and high quality product, probably better known to industrial users than in the small kitchen. It has little flavour and so makes a sound all-purpose oil. Use it in salad dressings, dips and so forth. However, on frying it can form a stiff 'varnish' which adheres firmly to the pan. It is precisely this quality which makes it ideal for use in making paints and varnishes. The oil is often processed to eliminate the 'varnish' before being used commercially as a frying oil or in the baking industry as a shortening.

Soya beans flourish in near-tropical conditions and the bumper harvests are in North and South America and China. From there the beans are shipped to Europe to be crushed in mills. Crude oil and meal for use in animal feeds are first produced, then comes the oil which is further refined to remove impurities and to improve the flavour. Lecithins, used commercially as emulsifiers, are a by-product.

Soya beans, which grow three or four in a pod, are in fact comparatively low in oil content. Yet soya is now the leading source of vegetable oil in the world.

Pine seed oil

This is a deluxe oil – with a price to match. Made in France from pine nuts, it is a delightful oil for salad dressing or for tossing vegetables. But it costs in the order of four times as much as rivals hazelnut and sesame oil which accounts for why it is so little used.

LEFT: GROUNDNUT OIL IS CLEAR IN COLOUR AND MILD TO TASTE.

BELOW: THE YIELD OF OIL FROM PINE NUTS IS COMPARATIVELY SMALL.

Walnut oil

With a flavour and pungency reminiscent of the nut itself, it is usually made in the Dordogne and Perigord regions of France and also in Italy. Production is small-scale and therefore it is pint-for-pint more expensive than most. The best quality walnut oil is supplied by gourmet shops, but there are cheaper varieties that lack the clarity of flavour. Walnut oil has a short shelf life. Keep it in a cool, dark place – it is one of the few oils that tolerates refrigeration. Use it in sauces, with pasta, for sautéing and in salad dressings.

Almond oil

There are two kinds of almonds, bitter and sweet. Oil is derived from pressing sweet almonds and collecting the yield. Surprisingly, it does not bear the flavour of almonds although there is a suggestion of nuttiness. French-made almond oil has the highest reputation, and its price reflects this. American almond oil is less flavoursome and is available much more cheaply. This oil is cholesterol-free with a high flash point. It is used for stir-fry and salad dressing although it is more ideally utilised in the making of confectionery. Often it is used for cosmetic purposes, and for years Europeans have rubbed it into dry skin to make it supple.

Hazelnut oil

This is a richly flavoured brown oil breathing the aroma of roasted hazelnuts which works beautifully with fish or in a marinade. Nutty oils are versatile and should be used sparingly and cold to get the best the bottle has to offer.

Palm oil

The palm yields two kinds of oil from its fruit. One is from the the pulp or pericarp which is found beneath the outer skin, and the other is from the nut or kernel at its heart. The first is flame-coloured with a flavour associated with West African or Brazilian cooking, while the more valuable oil from the kernel is pale yellow verging on white and is mild in character. Palm kernel oil is in effect split into two commodities. The first is oleine, a frying oil, and the second is stearin, which turns up in margarine and cosmetics. Both oils are unfashionably high in saturated fats but appear not to contain the so-called trans-fatty acids which are linked to heart disease. Palm oil is mostly produced in Malaysia and Indonesia.

Vegetable oil

Very much as it sounds, it is a blend of different vegetable oils.

Manufacturers tend to make up their own combinations. A single bottle may contain corn, soya, safflower, rapeseed or even coconut oil and diverse brands may be entirely different in composition. There's no breakdown on the label so consumers remain in the dark about precisely what they are using. There's very little flavour and aroma but it makes an economical workaday oil.

Fruit oil

Grate the rinds of grapefruit, lemons and sweet oranges and you can see the oils oozing out. Primarily their use is for cake or sauce making.

CITRUS OIL COMES FROM THE OUTER SKIN OF FRUITS.

OILS AROUND THE HOUSE

When it comes to buying oil it is all about making choices. Price is clearly a consideration but taste is equally important, as are the long-term health implications. Some oils have been refined, a process of five stages which consists of purification in a salt solution, neutralising to remove the fatty acids which might cause the oil to become rancid, bleaching to improve its colour, filtration and finally deodorising by steam distillation. Other oils are refreshingly untouched and pure. Make the right selection for you and your family after working out just how, why and when oil will be used. Think, too, about its other roles both in the kitchen and out. Oil is a worthy preservative, a beauty aid and can even be used for doing jobs around the house.

Culinary Uses

Oils may be used as a condiment, as an ingredient or as a method of cooking. Only the best oil deserves a place at the table where it may be used for drizzling on food or dipping bread.

RIGHT: MOST FOOD BENEFITS FROM A SPLASH OF OIL BEFORE BEING COOKED.

BELOW: FOOD IS SEALED BY HOT OIL DURING FRYING.

H owever, an oil in a stock, for example, which will be thoroughly heated may as well be an economy oil as the subtle flavours of the quality products are for the most part destroyed by cooking.

In cooking there are two primary methods of using oil – shallow and deep frying. The role of the oil is to transfer heat effectively to the food and thereby cook it. During shallow frying only part of the item is immersed, whereas in deep frying food is plunged into oil and heated until it reaches its smoking point, and the

cooking times are brief. Choice of oil is not paramount, in fact, the blander the better. The aim is that the oil should coat and seal food rather than be absorbed by it. That will only happen if the oil is adequately heated. Always test that the pan of oil for deep frying is sufficiently hot. Drop in a cube of bread and check to ensure that it floats and turns brown within a minute. If the bread sinks it is likely that the oil is too cool and the bread has absorbed it. If deep frying is done successfully the food does not take on the flavour of the oil and the calorific values are not immense.

Do not continually re-use oil which has been heated to smoking point. A chemical reaction within sizzling oil may render it toxic and dangerous for subsequent consumption. Discard it and start again with fresh oil.

Take care too that oil being used a second time is only used for cooking the same foodstuffs. For example, do not use oil that has been used for roasting meat a second time with fish.

Don't make the mistake of buying one medium quality oil to suit all purposes – this is a hopeless halfway-house. It is equally pointless using decent olive oil for cooking and mediocre sunflower oil for dressing. Buy oil cheaply in bulk for frying. When food is properly fried the taste of the oil does not impinge on the food. Invest in a fine tasting condiment oil, which is top grade and can be used to make dressing, for dipping bread or to drizzle over pastas, vegetables and grilled foods.

Pouring oil has about 120 calories in each tablespoon. Oils may be tagged as 'light' or even 'extra light', but this generally refers to flavour rather than calorific value.

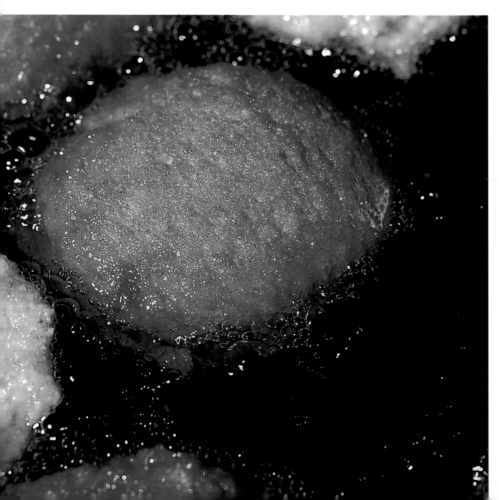

Preserving in Oil

Oil has long been used for preserving foodstuffs. The technique was recorded for posterity in the writings of the ancient Romans. Hot countries used pressed oils for food storage just as cold countries preserved in animal fat. Among the most familiar products stored in oil are tuna pieces, anchovies, goat's cheese, artichoke hearts and, of course, olives. Some foods, such as sun-dried tomatoes, even gain in flavour during the process.

In the Lebanon, aubergines are frequently preserved in oil, in Italy one finds chargrilled vegetables while in the Middle East the preference is for labna, which is soft yoghurt cheese. Food also assumes some of the nutrient values of the oil. Once goods stored in oil were considered luxury items, but the increasing accessibility of good-quality oil has made this less so today.

It is a simple procedure to preserve foods in oil in the kitchen. However, making the right choice of food is important. Items containing plenty of water are never a good option until as much of the liquid as possible has been removed. Do this by salting for olives and lemons or by cooking for mushrooms. Feta and goat's cheese needs no such attention.

Choose wide-necked jars for storage and make sure they are sterilised by washing, rinsing and placing either in boiling water or on a tray in the oven. Place the food inside, making sure there is a margin at the top so none is left exposed. Pour over the oil until the food is covered.

Olive oil is a better medium than extra virgin olive oil as the taste is much milder. Sunflower oil is equally adequate but avoid the less robust types like nut oils as these are unlikely to endure. Consider combining two oils – extra virgin olive oil and groundnut oil – to get the best of both. To avoid the risk of the oil turning rancid take it from a newly opened bottle.

Seal the jars with rust-free screw top lids and keep them in a dark, cool place. Do not use for at least a week to taste the benefit of the oil. Food stored in this way is unlikely to keep any longer than three months.

Once the preserved items have been eaten don't forget to use the remaining oil. It will have assumed the flavour of the foodstuffs which were in it so utilise it appropriately, either in cooking or for salad dressings.

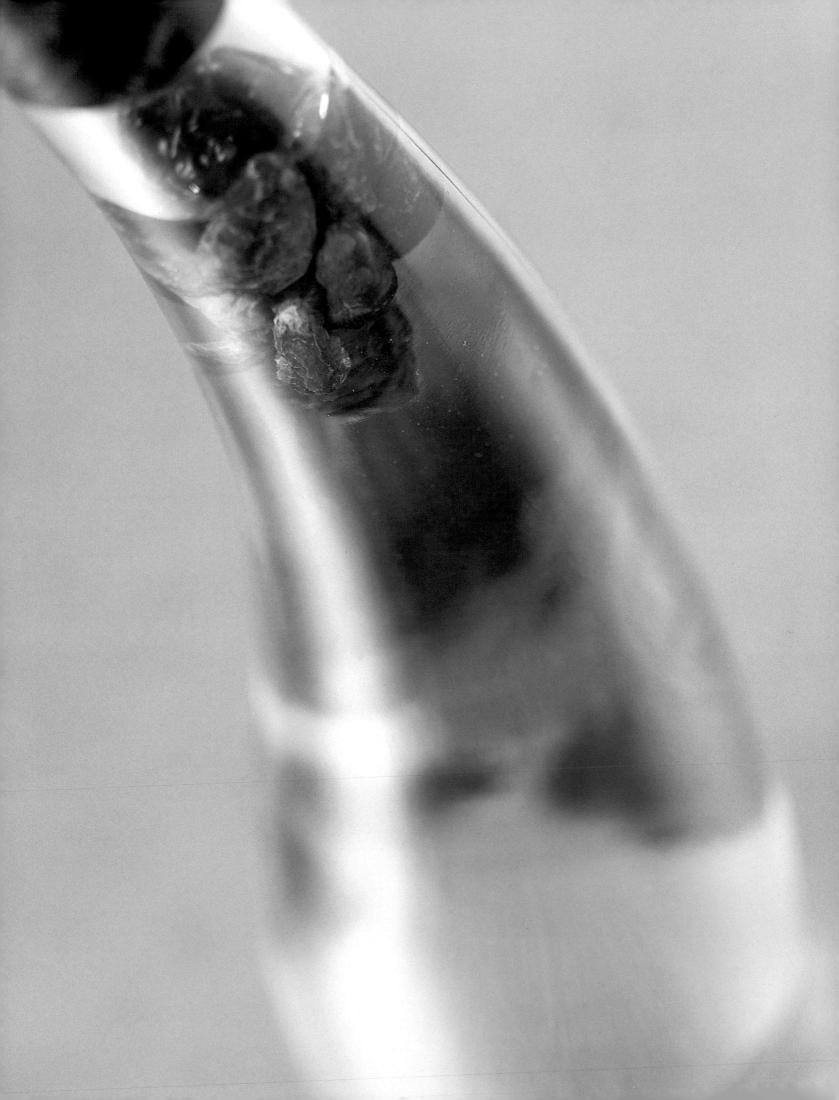

Flavoured Oils

Flavoured oils are now big news in the kitchen, a trend that has come in the wake of the olive oil revolution. Within a decade a trickle of speciality oils leaving the gourmet shops has become a tide.

Oils can be infused with herbs, mushrooms, even truffles. Don't cook with infused oils but add at or near the end of cooking. Otherwise the risk of destroying the subtle delicacies of taste is colossal. They can be used where cream and butter would once have been the natural choice. Oil is lighter than butter and more flavoursome. Such is the popularity of infused oils that some chefs have been accused of over-using them.

It is possible to make your own infused oils. Try putting herbs or sundried tomatoes in a lightly-flavoured olive oil and then keep it over a low heat – a bain-marie would be suitable – for eight hours to release the flavours. For spices take the same approach but use a plain-tasting oil like groundnut. Dry roast the spices before combining with oil to achieve a better flavour. Crushing the spices also unleashes flavour. Safflower, sunflower, corn and canola are ideal oils for infusion, being devoid of taste, so the flavour of whatever has been added will shine through. Those oils with pungent flavours of their own are less appropriate, not least on grounds of cost. So avoid using the nut oils and palm oil.

The joy of using rare and expensive foodstuffs to infuse is that the life of a costly commodity is extended. It is possible to make a luxury oil with just the shavings of a truffle. An ingredient which might have been used in one meal can then be used to impart the inimitable flavour in many more.

Some infused oils are difficult to replicate. Basil is notoriously tricky to infuse at home, mainly because the water content is high. Even top chefs will buy basil oil which is sometimes marketed under the name 'extra pesto' oil.

The peril of buying infused oils is that customers could be deceived into buying cheap oils with food essences added, believing them to be professionally infused oils. There is also a health risk involved when garlic is infused. Two outbreaks of botulism in Canada and the United States during the 1980s were traced back to chopped garlic in oil. Now it is advised that garlic is acidified before being immersed in oil.

A similar effect to garlic-infused oil can be achieved by crushing a clove of garlic around the rim of a salad bowl.

LEFT: CHILLI OIL CAN GREATLY ENHANCE THE FLAVOUR OF A MEAL WITH ITS PEPPERY TASTE.

BELOW: SPICES SHOULD BE DRY ROASTED BEFORE BEING COMBINED WITH OIL.

Cosmetic Qualities

The age of aromatherapy has brought with it a new aspect on oils. Selected culinary oils are a vital part of the aromatherapy process in which scented plant extracts are mixed with essential oils and applied in massage.

C ulinary oils form the base to which both the fragrant extracts and the essential oils are added. Their bountiful merits are taken through the skin rather than by

RIGHT: HANDS STAY SOFT IF THEY ARE COATED IN A LIGHT CULINARY OIL.

OLIVE OIL CAN BE THE LIFE AND 'SOLE' OF A BEAUTY REGIME.

mouth. The most suitable are the cold pressed oils which bear little or no smell and are 100 percent pure. An aromatherapist is therefore most likely to make purchases in the local health shop instead of the supermarket.

Almond oil is a sound base, rich in protein and very nourishing. It is an excellent choice as it stores well. It can also be made into a cold cream by blending with white wax and rosewater. Incidentally, any rancid oil is as undesirable for massage as it is for cooking.

More expensive than almond oil and more delicate is apricot kernel oil which is gentle enough to be used on just about any face. Grapeseed oil is fine, clear and comparatively non-greasy. It is reputed to make even well-weathered faces feel smooth again.

Hazelnut oil penetrates the skin quickly and deeply. Not only is it nourishing but it stimulates circulation and is therefore good for muscular problems. For acne, jojoba oil – squeezed from the jojoba nut – is advised. Like almond oil it is slow to become rancid.

Olive oil appears as beneficial for the body on the outside as it is on the inside. It is said by the optimistic to delay the effects of human ageing, further it is helpful for rheumatism and for undue itching of the skin. A simple cleanser can be made from a beaten egg mixed with olive oil. Spread it over the face then wash off with warm water and cotton wool. It is most appropriate for dry skins. To strengthen weak nails soak them in warm olive oil for five minutes twice daily. Afterwards gently push back the cuticles. The disadvantage of using olive oil is its distinctive smell.

Sesame oil is another oil with excellent staying power and can be used for treating skin disorders such as eczema and psoriasis. Soya oil is a popular choice for massage as it doesn't become sticky.

Although sunflower oil doesn't keep well it is rich in vitamin E which is vital for cell membrane repair.

Other oils to be used in conjunction with those above include avocado oil, which has a similar profile to almond oil; calendular oil, recommended for chapped skin; vividly coloured carrot oil which is reputed to tone and rejuvenate skin; evening primrose oil, which tackles scaly skin; and wheatgerm oil, a valuable anti-oxidant which will lend longevity to the base oil and is rich in vitamin E. It is ideal for the more mature skin.

But using oils on the skin is nothing new. The Egyptians used oils for cosmetic purposes and during the embalming process. In ancient Greece olive oil was used medicinally to cure ailments both internally and externally. Hippocrates (ca. 460–377 BC), the pioneering Greek physician, used to prescribe olive oil as a therapeutic. Religious leaders were anointed with it, as were kings.

ABOVE: THE GOODNESS OF OILS USED IN BEAUTY PREPARATIONS IS ABSORBED THROUGH THE SKIN.

Household Uses

The Chinese put cooking oil to good use. Their most valued cooking utensil, the wok, is prone to rust. Chinese cooks spread a drop of oil inside their wok and heat it to create a thin, protective layer across the surface, which will prevent rust from setting in. The same method can be used with western pans, and a non-stick surface will also benefit from a drop of oil between uses.

The frustration of having a beautifully polished dark wood table ruined by white rings – the imprint of a carelessly placed glass or cup – is familiar to everyone. But this tell-tale sign can be eradicated quickly and cheaply in a short-cut method once known to butlers everywhere. Simply mix cigarette or cigar ash with vegetable oil and apply to the rogue marks. Some may take more rubbing than others but the age-old remedy has worked for generations. It is only advisable for dark woods, however. Where there are marks on light wood use an oily brazil nut.

Linseed oil, the product of flax, was loved by the Victorian housekeepers who used it for furniture, floors and much more. Linseed oil is particularly beneficial in the care of teak and other hard woods. Choose boiled linseed oil for the purpose. To achieve an even spread soak cotton wool with linseed oil then wrap it in a clean rag. Another use is in the protection of wood floors.

Antique furniture may be revived with a mixture of two parts turpentine, two parts methylated spirits, two parts vinegar and one part raw linseed oil. Put all the constituents into a bottle and shake. Use infrequently and always test on a small, hidden patch before wholesale use. Cricket lovers treat their bats to repeated doses of linseed oil, sanding lightly in between each layer.

An ideal polish for leather is quickly made with the combination of lanoline and either neatsfoot oil – available from saddlers – or linseed oil. It can be used in small quantities on leather book bindings, belts, handbags and tack.

The early Egyptians used olive oil for fuel in lamps. Unless cash supplies are unlimited this is not an ideal choice today. But if necessary cooking oils could be used in lamps. Use vinegar to clean the wicks before lighting as this will stop unnecessary smoking.

YOU CAN KEEP A WOK IN TOP CONDITION BY SPREADING OIL INSIDE AND HEATING IT AFTER USE.

VINEGARS

Vinegar has a long and noble heritage which goes hand in glove with another tradition beloved by man since the Dark Ages – drinking alcohol. That's because vinegar was the happy accident that occurred when brewing missed the mark. Most of us think of vinegar as an inferior to beers, wines or spirits. Only the enlightened few actively seek out this fermented product to enjoy in its own right. Just like alcoholic drinks, the variation in character and quality is vast. At the top of the range there are the chic balsamics while in the lower echelons lurk the dreary distilled forms, better suited for washing windows than splashing on salad. However, as with oils, it's the taste factor that conquers all.

Wine Vinegar

It seems that every country or region has a vinegar to call its own. In essence it is the local brew turned sour, an entirely natural process when the level of alcohol which would otherwise preserve it falls below 18 percent. The term vinegar is a perversion of the French term 'vin aigre', or 'sour wine'.

The first record of vinegar appears 2,000 years BC in Egypt. It is also known that Roman legions drank Posca, a soured red wine. In England King Charles II (1630–85) was known to enjoy 'winiger' on his salad. The Victorians of 19th century Britain added fruit vinegars to water for a refreshing summer drink.

However, the vinegar trade lacked the excitement and allure of some other foodstuffs. This is being overcome, not least by the reputation of balsamic vinegar. American Lawrence Diggs, bowled over by what he calls 'sour power', has launched the organisation 'Vinegar Connoisseurs International' in an attempt to increase the role of vinegar in the kitchen and around the house.

All vinegars have a common process in which there are two fermentations. In the first, yeast converts the sugar of the brew to alcohol much the same as it would in any brewing procedure. In vinegar production the resulting liquor is called gyle. Its alcoholic strength is usually between six and nine percent.

The next step is the second fermentation at which point the system parts company with brewing of beverages. This time it is done in the presence of an Acetobactor, or aerobic bacteria. It is the role of the bacteria to convert the alcohol into acetic acid, the very substance which gives vinegar its keen taste.

In the act of converting alcohol to vinegar a so-called mother is created, a skin which covers the surface of the liquid like a scum. This is simply a layer of yeast and bacteria – although it's none too appetising to look at.

Just like the art of brewing, making vinegar is a natural process but success is by no means guaranteed. If the fermentation is not closely supervised the end product might be bitter or lacking in any discernible flavour.

Wine vinegar must have a level of six percent acetic acid to conform with the accepted standards. It is made from red, rose and white wine but no longer has a flavour similar to wine. It is produced in Italy and Spain but the finest come from France.

The Orleans method practised in the Loire valley in France is recognised to be the highest quality of wine vinegar in the world. It is distinguished by a lengthy fermentation which takes place in oak barrels at 21 degrees centigrade or 70 degrees fahrenheit – just about room temperature. Of course, the price reflects the greater length of time devoted to making Orleans-style vinegar and it has a certain rarity value. The taste is superior to most of its rivals, but sadly, few people ever get the opportunity to sample it.

Among its competitors in the arena of wine vinegars is pale Champagne vinegar, which has the kudos of its sparkling drinks partner, and the more full-bodied Rioja. In America Zinfandel wine vinegar is emerging as a quality product. Another fine vinegar with a contrasting character is sherry vinegar which in its manufacture mirrors the world-famous sherry product. It is warmly rich, coming as it does from the wooden casks in which the drink is brewed. Given the choice it would be wise to use a quality Orleans vinegar on its own so its taste can be fully appreciated but the less remarkable wine vinegars blend well with other ingredients.

Cider Vinegar

To the drinker, the autumn orchard lined with trees dripping with apples speaks of cider by the flagon. To the foodie the same sight says cider vinegar, the fruity, straw-coloured by-product of the cider-making industry. It is a versatile, sharp-flavoured all-purpose vinegar, a cut above its rival malt vinegar both in flavour and in price.

CIDER VINEGAR IS A FRUITY CONDIMENT IDEAL FOR USE IN CHUTNIES AND FRUIT PICKLING.

Apples which are suitable for making cider and vinegar are often not appropriate for eating. The flesh is hard and the taste is unpleasantly tart. Such apples only come into their own when they are fermented with sugar. When the orchards are stripped the fruit is taken to a plant where the apples are mechanically squeezed to extract the juice. The liquid goes into large oak vats or the stainless steel equivalent and the first fermentation takes place. With cider this is not a speedy process and can take anything between four weeks and six months.

The acetification then occurs in a vat stacked with sterilised birch twigs previously soaked in alcohol and vinegar. For three weeks the apple juice will be pumped around to allow an even distribution of the acetobactor. When the vinegar has been completed it is bottled, often with a preservative like Ascorbic acid (Vitamin C) added. The practise of using sulphites for this purpose is dying out.

Thanks to its apple flavour cider vinegar is ideal for pickling fruit and for use in chutnies, where it complements the food it is alongside.

In the latter half of the 19th century it was one of the main ingredients in vinegar pie, a dish that has been all but forgotten. This was made when fruit was scarce and was popular in French Canada, the American Midwest and the Deep South. To make it cider vinegar was boiled with water then poured onto a mixture of sugar, salt, flour and beaten egg yolks and cooked in a pan. Butter and lemon extract was added before the thickened liquid was poured into a pastry case. Beaten egg whites were put on top and the pie was cooked in a slow oven.

Cider vinegar, along with wine vinegar, often falls victim to cloudiness during storage and may even take on dark hues. This is a sign that iron in the vinegar has combined with the tannins, the property that gives vinegar its sharp flavour. This is particularly likely to occur if the vinegar has been stored in a clear bottle and exposed to light. Vinegar also darkens as it ages, but fortunately the flavour is not impaired, and cloudy vinegar can be used in the normal way.

CIDER VINEGAR IS PRODUCED IN REGIONS RICH WITH ORCHARDS AND IS MADE IN AMERICA, BRITAIN AND FRANCE.

A CIDER PRESS.

Malt Vinegar

Malt vinegar is made from barley which has been malted, a process by which it is steeped in water, sprouted and then dried in a kiln. It's a challenging task, generally left to specialist maltsters who work out of professional malt houses.

Once giant stone mills were used to crush the malt. These days the job is done by steel rollers which of course are very efficient. When it leaves the mill the ground malt is mashed with hot water as the temperature is increased. The starch in the malt becomes a sugar called maltose which dissolves. The liquor that is formed at this stage, called wort, drains away from the mash into a fermenter.

The first fermentation for malt vinegar is rapid and the resulting gyle is highly alcoholic. It is pumped into storage vats where it remains for several months while the yeast settles. Then it is time for the gyle to undergo acetification. Again, birch twigs are used to aid the process. Once this would happen naturally with barrels lined up outside over a period of at least five months.

Today acetifiers do the same job in five days. There is a period in which the vinegar is matured before being bottled and dispatched to shops.

In its natural form malt vinegar is light in colour but it is often darkened with the addition of caramel. Malt vinegar is used for piccalilli pickle, pickled walnuts and pickled onions. Sometimes malt vinegar may be sold with pickling spices already incorporated into it. The spices may be any or all of the following: allspice, bay leaves, cardamom, cayenne pepper, chillies, cinnamon, cloves, coriander seeds, ginger, mustard, peppercorns, turmeric.

One of the most respected vinegar brand names is Sarson's, the product of a company established in 1794 by Thomas Sarson. His son Henry James conjured up the curious product name of Sarson's Virgin Vinegar, a name emblazoned on bottles until the 1950s. Only then was the word 'virgin' finally abandoned for its inappropriate imagery. Today Sarson's is part of food conglomerate Nestlé although it retains its name.

Malt vinegar is too strong to use as a dressing but makes a wonderful condiment for fried food and is best known in northern Europe as an accompaniment to fish and chips.

Unfortunately, the bottles purporting to be vinegar which furnish many fast-food outlets are often non-brewed condiment. Rather than vinegar they are actually a solution of acetic acid between four to eight percent in strength coloured by caramel. This is made as a by-product of the petro-chemical industry!

Balsamic Vinegar

An aristocrat among vinegars, this intriguing, dark brew comes only from Modena, northern Italy, and is revered there every bit as much as the city's 11th century Romanesque cathedral and its ancient palaces and university. It's not so much a vinegar, more of a smooth, soothing balm – hence the name.

The Balsamics are not derived from sour wine but from a must, or newly pressed grape juice which is boiled and filtered. To be precise, it is from the Trebbiano grape which flourishes in the Modena region.

Balsamic vinegar differs from others because there is no fermentation process in the early stages so the sugar remains intact. During boiling, however, the must will reduce between thirty and seventy percent, depending on its sugar content.

Thereafter it is aged in barrels made of oak, chestnut, juniper or cherry, ash and finally mulberry – transferring from one to another at regular intervals. These barrels are kept warm with a low flame to distil the vinegar further by a process of evaporation and subsequent barrels are smaller than the first to accommodate a diminishing liquid. Thus the oak cask has a capacity of 60 litres while the mulberry barrel, used when the process is completing, holds just 20 litres. So the quantities made are never huge. The barrels are never cleaned for clinging to the sides is the bacterial 'mother' which causes the fermentation process.

The transfer of vinegar from one barrel to the next is a process known as 'rincalzo' and frequently it takes place in the spring. For the families involved it is something of a ritual and the traditional methods involved vary. To these families the barrels – which are

BALSAMIC VINEGAR IS A CLASS APART FROM ITS RIVALS. IT IS BREWED FROM GRAPES GROWN AROUND MODENA IN ITALY.

years old – are central to the business and their worth to the vinegar maker is inestimable. There's further anecdotal evidence which claims there are bottles of balsamic vinegar in the cellars of the families which produced them which date back more than 100 years. The value of these is phenomenal.

The product that remains is a moody fluid with an exquisite taste. Expensive, yes, but it goes a long way. The taste is strong so balsamics can be used sparingly.

Vintage

It is the job of the Master Tasters to determine when the vinegar is ready for bottling.

The Maestri Assaggiatori di Modena or Master Tasters of Modena decree that:

- The traditional balsamic vinegar is obtained from the boiled must of grapes which is subjected to a long process of natural fermentation and concentration.
- This is to be effected over an exceptionally long ageing period in a succession of barrels made of various types of wood, strictly without the addition of aromatic substances.
- Of a lively, brown colour it should manifest a molasses-like consistency, a mildly acidic nose which is at once penetrating and agreeable.
- The traditional taste is a smooth, subtle interplay of sweet and sour flavours. It is a full, rich taste in complete harmony with the olfactory (aromatic) properties.

Balsamic vinegars have a vintage structure. The junior members of the family are between eight and ten years old and are ideal for using with salad or adding to gravies. Intermediates are between 15 and 20 years old. Savour them with wafer-thin slices of Parmesan, or perhaps with fried food, salt cod or raw fish. There's a home for this type of balsamic vinegar with honey and mustard in dressing. Never be tempted to mask its taste with garlic and herbs – it needs no assistance in yielding flavour.

Senior in the ranks is the vinegar 'aceto extravecchio', matured for 25 years or more. It is dark but not heavy, fragrant without being musky, smooth with a syrupy texture. So fine is this vinegar it may be served after a meal in the place of a liqueur! It is also a wonderful complement to strawberries. Dribble on the red fruits and leave to macerate for 30 minutes. Likewise, it is dazzling when it is drizzled on home-made vanilla ice-cream.

Supreme specimens of vinegar once formed part of a dowry for a bride, and it costs more than an average Champagne. It is essential, then, to taste balsamic vinegar by the drop rather than the spoonful. For those who invest or indulge in the most expensive of balsamics a spout which will release the precious liquid from the bottle drop by drop is a must.

LEFT: BALSAMIC VINEGAR IS DELICIOUS ON FRESH SCROLLS OF PARMESAN CHEESE.

SO DELICATE IS THE FLAVOUR, BALSAMIC VINEGAR CAN BE SERVED WITH STRAWBERRIES.

Varieties

Buyer beware! There are two standards of balsamic vinegar available, and traditional makers of balsamic vinegar have become concerned about the growing popularity of the industrial version. Producers have seized on the name but embrace none of the time-honoured methods of production in their pursuit of a quick turnover. Specifically they bypass the lengthy ageing process which is at the very heart of balsamic vinegar production. This has become all the more acute as balsamic vinegar is no longer the culinary secret of northern Italy. Its reputation has spread worldwide – although intimate knowledge of the product has followed in its wake at a much slower pace. Unquestioning consumers are easily taken in when they buy lookalike products which compare favourably in price with the traditional brands.

Accordingly, the Consorzio Produttori Aceto Balsamico Tradizionale di Modena, a group which looks after the interests of traditional balsamic vinegar, has issued its own label which old-style balsamic vinegar may bear on its bottle. The label has the words 'Aceto Balsamico Tradizionale di Modena' beneath two shields and buyers can then rest assured that the contents are at least 12 years old.

Lawrence Diggs is full of praise for balsamic: 'The Traditionale is an incredible product. It has secondary and tertiary tastes. It unfolds as you sample it. Other products are not so delicate. This is the kind of vinegar you have to sip to appreciate.'

But he warns also of the dangers for unsuspecting buyers: 'Producers could even be using boiled down Coca-Cola syrup. They put acetic acid with it and, as long as it looks brown and thick and has a kind of sweet and sour taste, that will work for many people. The reason is that many people will never try the real thing.

'Consumers are to blame. They demand a certain product at a certain price. If they don't get it from one supplier they will move on to the next. People are not prepared to pay the real price for well-produced food.'

LOOK FOR THE LABEL WHICH DISTINGUISHES VINTAGE BALSAMIC VINEGAR FROM ITS 'QUICK FIX' RIVALS.

Rice Vinegar

Rice vinegars from China and Japan are set to become tomorrow's balsamics. Like the vinegar men of Modena, oriental makers have kept their products mostly hidden from the rest of the world. Observers, including expert Lawrence Diggs, believes the obscurity will be short lived:

'The Chinese have a superb grain vinegar from Shanxi. This is somewhere close to a balsamic at nowhere near the price. This is going to be the next rage', predicts Diggs.

Vinegar has been made in the Shanxi province of China for nearly 3,000 years. It is known that brewing had begun by 770 BC – the date may have even been earlier – and became so widespread that records reveal most householders made their own. The area of Shanxi, close to Mongolia, has remained remote. The first road linking Shanxi and the country's capital, Beijing, was only completed in 1996. Despite stirrings of interest in the locally made vinegar, producers are keeping the exact recipe and the procedures they follow close to their chests.

It is known that Shanxi vinegar is made from a mash of sorghum, which is a tropical cereal grass, barley and peas. At some stage the mother is added. A staggering fact is that the mother is part of the same bacterial mass used hundreds, maybe thousands, of years ago. Like all mothers it is skimmed from the top of the vinegar and transferred to the next batch.

While the mother gets to work the vinegar is in an urn which itself dates back to antiquity. It is left outside in the sunshine for a year, during which time harmful bacteria are killed off. The result is a dark maroon-coloured vinegar with a sweet flavour, sufficiently palatable to be drunk before a meal, as is the habit in Shanxi. But there's an underlying tang which rivals the

honeyed flavours to provide a taste experience. The people of Shanxi firmly believe that the product is more than merely a condiment. It is thanks to the vinegar that they enjoy health and long life, they claim.

Of course, there are other varieties of vinegar hailing from China, and some more from Japan, many of which have rice as a basic ingredient. Most rice vinegars are a clear, straw colour although there is a variety which has rich muddy tones that is made from whole brown rice.

Chinese vinegars are characteristically sharp and sour. They are often substituted in western recipes with cider vinegar. From Japan comes softer and more mellow varieties often used for making sushi, the raw fish delicacy. Rice vinegars are quite different from soy sauce. Both are the product of fermentations but the latter is made from soy beans.

Spirit vinegar

The most potent of the bunch, spirit vinegar still contains alcohol when it is bottled. Its main value is for pickling, the flavour being far too savage for it to be used as a condiment.

LEFT: CHINESE VINEGAR MAKERS KEEP THEIR PROCEDURES A SECRET.

Flavoured Vinegars

Vinegars are finding a new lease of life with a fashion to flavour them with herbs, fruits and so forth. The aim is to make them look as good as they taste and the technique for creating them is astonishingly simple.

BOTTLES OF FLAVOURED VINEGAR CAN BE VISUALLY ATTRACTIVE.

F irstly, choose a flavouring. Woody herbs like rosemary and tarragon are always popular. Any of the soft fruits, including raspberries and blackberries, will make a sensational combination with wine or cider vinegar as will citrus fruits. Garlic is another option, ideal for making dressings, while seaweed is among the newest, most exotic available. Indeed, the options for flavouring vinegars seem almost endless.

Herb vinegars

Adding herbs to make flavoured vinegars could not be easier. Select a sprig of the chosen herb – or a variety – and, using the flat blade of a knife bruise the foliage to release the flavour. Pop it into a sterilised bottle then pour over the vinegar until it reaches the top. Make sure that you use vinegar with an acetic acid content of more than five percent. Seal the bottles tightly with non-corrosive screw-top lids or even corks which can be hammered into the neck of the bottle after being soaked in boiling water. If the herb sprig looks tired after a short period then replace it with another.

Fruit vinegars

The process of making a fruit vinegar is not much more demanding. Put a half pint of wine vinegar into a bowl and add one pound or half a kilo of fresh fruit. Crush at least some of the fruit to extract maximum flavour. Leave the fruit steeped in vinegar for four days. Then strain it into a measuring jug and put into a pan. Boil the strained vinegar for 10 minutes and then it is ready to bottle. Once again use sterile bottles and seal with air-tight lids. Fruit vinegars go particularly well with rich meats like game and in dressings.

Flavoured vinegar does improve on standing although it should be used within a year. Keep an eye on the flavoured vinegar in case it begins to ferment. That may happen if the bottle is stored in a warm place. At the first sign of fermentation throw the bottle away. Vinegar may evaporate if bottles are not properly sealed.

An ideal gift

Home-made flavoured vinegar makes a great gift. Use an attractive bottle or a plain one which you could decorate yourself by painting or by use of ribbons. Invest in some embellished labels and a calligraphy pen. You could even tie swatches of hessian or coloured material around the top and neck of the bottle. If you are short of ideas, peruse the shelves of a local department store where items like these are sold.

WHEN BOTTLING ONE OF THE MORE EXPENSIVE VINEGARS, IT IS A GOOD IDEA TO CHOOSE A BOTTLE WITH A TAP SO THAT THE PRECIOUS LIQUID CAN BE DISPENSED SPARINGLY.

VINEGARS AROUND THE HOUSE

Distinctive by flavour, vinegar may not be to everyone's taste. Even the smoothest and most sophisticated of the species retains a hint of tartness. It is that very trait which makes it such an effective preserver of foods. However, if there's no place for vinegar in the kitchen it still deserves houseroom for its astonishing domestic diversity.

Pickling in Vinegar

Pickling is something of a neglected art. In the days before cans, freezers and fast food it was a crucial method of preserving food particularly after an abundant harvest when excess would otherwise have gone to waste. Thanks to the marvellous preserving powers of vinegar winter mealtimes were brightened with the crunchy, colourful, zesty fare plucked the previous summer. In the most hostile of eras it was even a way of avoiding hunger or famine. Pickling, along with salting, was also one of the few ways that food from other regions, even overseas, could be enjoyed by those in different climates and cultures.

RIGHT: GHERKINS FOUND IN PICKLES ARE IMMATURE CUCUMBERS.

One of the first to publish a work on pickling was Mrs Hannah Glasse who related her techniques in 1747 in the book 'Domestic Cookery Made Easy'. In fact the process had been a kitchen ritual for some 1,500 years before that. Romans were prolific picklers. Using sizeable terracotta pots they put down the culinary spoils of the empire into vinegar, oil and brine. Some fruits were kept in honey.

Pickling saves food from decomposition by bacteria, yeasts and moulds. It does so by creating conditions in which the damaging organisms are unable to grow.

BELOW: VEGETABLES SHOULD BE BRINED BEFORE PICKLING TO REDUCE THEIR WATER CONTENT.

There are few vegetables that cannot be pickled. Apart from the commonplace pickled onions the connoisseur may choose beetroot, cabbage – red and white – mushrooms, artichokes, cauliflowers, cucumbers... the list goes on. Even fruits can be successfully pickled. Pears, plums and damsons from pickling jars are a fine relish for hot meat. Peaches too can be preserved for savoury consumption although they may benefit from being doused in a sweetened vinegar. Cook fruit in a light syrup before committing them to vinegar.

Only fruit or vegetables in peak condition can be successfully pickled. Trim using a stainless steel knife so that all bruises and deteriorating flesh is removed. Vegetables which have been lightly steamed are ready to be pickled. Raw vegetables must be salted first to extract some of the water within them and to allow the vinegar to fully penetrate – if water remains in the vegetables it can dilute the vinegar, so inhibiting its preserving capabilities. If the brining time has not been long enough the vinegar is likely to cloud, so don't skimp on the brining times. Choose sea salt for the purpose as table salt may have chemical additives in it.

There are two ways of brining. Dry brining means the vegetables are stacked in a large, non-metallic bowl with salt between each layer. Leave overnight, stirring occasionally. In wet brining the vegetables are left standing overnight in a solution of salt and water. After both procedures the vegetables should be rinsed and patted dry. Always avoid using metal utensils.

After cooking or brining the vegetables commit them to dry, sterile jars or bottles. Remember, the vinegar must have access to every part of the jar so don't pack everything in too tightly. Likewise, don't fill the jar to the rim. Leave an inch gap so that there is a margin of vinegar on top. When putting the produce into jars spare a thought for how it will all look, too. Neatly ordered stacks appear very attractive on the shelf.

Carefully pour vinegar over the produce and don't stop until it is covered. Release trapped air bubbles inside by gently tapping the side of the jar. Be sure to use vinegar that has at least five percent acetic strength or it will not have enough preserving powers.

Some pickles will float to the top of the jar after the vinegar has been added and remain stubbornly there, exposed to the air. Simply add a piece of crumpled greaseproof paper before putting the lid on and it will keep the pickles submerged until they absorb sufficient amounts of vinegar to weigh them down. The greaseproof paper may be removed within two weeks.

Seal pickle jars with rust-proof lids which have a screw fitting. Store the assembled jars in a dark, cool, dry cupboard. Pickles are ready to eat within two or three weeks but will be all the more flavoursome if they are left for several months. Keep an eye on the level of vinegar, however. If it drops simply top it up.

Yellow spots sometimes appear on pickled onions. While this spoils their appearance the substance formed is harmless.

Make Your Own Vinegar

Lawrence Diggs spends considerable amounts of time taking the mystique out of making vinegar. As he quickly points out there was a time when everybody made their own vinegar and thought nothing of it. That was particularly so in rural countries like Italy. Only when the price plummeted with the arrival of mass-produced vinegar did the impetus to 'do it yourself' disappear.

It is more than a simply a case of letting a wine or beer go sour. The aim is to make good quality vinegar which will not only rival shop-bought varieties but will exceed them in taste.

Use a container with a spout if possible. Make sure it is glass or stainless steel or the vinegar may be spoiled by a chemical reaction with it. Its size is of course dependent on how much vinegar you are intending to make.

Take a quantity of fresh fruit juice (avoid bottled juices because these may have been chemically treated with preservatives) and a similar amount of a starter culture. This is a technical term for the bacteria which will make vinegar. Either visit a store which specialises in home brewing or simply use a ready-made bottle of unpasteurised vinegar.

Put the two together in the container and keep it in a warm, dark place. The liquid must be exposed to air for the process to be successful, but it will attract insects so needs a muslim cover or similar.

Keep tasting the liquid until it suits your palate and then bottle it. It is possible to remedy shortcomings of home-made vinegar by adding shop bought vinegar in limited amounts. This will enhance the work of the bacteria. The end result will be smoother if it is stored for six months. Cheap wines can be turned into vinegar with this method. If you choose to make alcohol and then vinegar you will need brewing equipment to complete that first stage. There is no need for a 'mother' of vinegar at this level. This is better utilised for larger quantities of vinegar made by the experienced vinegar brewer.

The advantage of making vinegar at home is the superior flavour. It is done using the original slow process which large manufacturers have had to sacrifice for the sake of economies of scale. Also, it is a source of satisfaction to know precisely what the ingredients are when additions like colourings or caramel are standard ingredients used to 'improve' the appearance of commercial products.

'With a little bit of effort a person can make a nice vinegar,' explains Diggs. 'There is plenty of room for the distilled product and the quickly made product in the market place. Use it for window cleaning or athlete's foot. But please don't put it on your salad.' His tip for those who buy ready-made vinegar is to flavour it with herbs and spices or even a bit of roasted wood.

FAR LEFT: INGREDIENTS FOR SPICED VINEGAR.

LEFT: A BOTTLE OF BARREL-AGED VINEGAR.

Vinegar for Health

Mighty claims have been made for vinegar and its role in the pursuit of good health. Cider vinegar is a folklore favourite, perhaps because it comes from rural areas where healing with natural products was more widely accepted and adopted. Some of the boasts about vinegar stand up to scrutiny, others appear distinctly flakey. Science has barely delved into the arena, so much of the 'evidence' is anecdotal.

Vinegar's reputation for easing and healing burns is enduring. In the unfortunate event of a bad burn the advice is to pour on cider vinegar in generous quantities. It is said to not only stop the pain but to accelerate the process of healing. Believers advocate keeping a bottle in the kitchen and in the car for just such eventualities. Vinegar is consequently credited with having saved the lives of countless soldiers during wartime.

Likewise, it can be used to alleviate the discomfort of sunburn. As an anti-inflammatory measure it may also be helpful to those suffering from insect bites and shingles.

For years vinegar has been used to soothe sore throats, in the form of a gargle, and coughs. The acid condition created by vinegar is thought to prevent harmful bacteria from multiplying. It is also used to conquer nerves, insomnia, asthma, constipation, diarrhoea and cramp – although the rationale behind these claims is difficult to fathom. Nevertheless, whether it works merely as a placebo or in its own right vinegar provides an inexpensive remedy.

Vinegar can be hard to swallow on its own. It is taken more palatably with a teaspoonful of honey.

VINEGAR HAS LONG BEEN THOUGHT TO HAVE MANY QUALITIES WHICH CAN ASSIST WITH EXTERNAL WOUNDS AND INTERNAL AFFLICTIONS.

Vinegar and honey together are held to be a remedy for the effects of hay fever. Hiccoughs were once 'cured' with vinegar and brown sugar.

Less certain are the uses of vinegar in slimming and for arthritis. It is suggested in some quarters that two teaspoonfuls of cider vinegar in water in the morning and with meals will result in steady weight loss. One successful user allegedly commented: 'Cider vinegar is a girth's best friend'. However, that cider vinegar is an antidote to cream cakes and lack of exercise seems doubtful! The common sense rules of eating sensibly, exercising, avoiding smoking and cutting stress still apply.

The case for arthritis is unclear. There's a body of opinion which says cider vinegar counteracts the effects of this debilitating condition. However, Lawrence Diggs warns against investing too much hope in the cider vinegar remedy: 'To date there is no scientific evidence of any kind that vinegar cocktail will cure or relieve the pain of arthritis. I should mention also that it doesn't seem that scientists are all that interested in providing evidence either.

'If we ask ourselves how vinegar works in the body to cure arthritis we find it hard to come up with an explanation which will endure objective questioning.'

Cosmetic Qualities

Vinegar is every bit as efficacious on hair as its close relation beer. The vogue for beer shampoos and conditioners to achieve a healthy, shiny head of hair has passed. However, there are those who feel cider vinegar is as good, if not better, than beer, particularly for adding a sheen to dark hair.

RIGHT: ROSEMARY CAN BE ADDED TO VINEGAR TO MASK THE AROMA.

It is said vinegar will restore the natural balance between the scalp and hair if applied during the final rinse. This extends to dealing with dandruff. Another effect reported by the users of cider vinegar is an improvement in the appearance of their skin. While the claims stop short of it being a wrinkle-eraser there is common consent that skin tone

APPLY VINEGAR TO THE HAIR AND SCALP DURING THE FINAL RINSE.

improves. If you believe that inner cleanliness is reflected in a healthy complexion then seeking fitness through taking vinegar may have a positive effect.

Vinegar is also said to remove age spots, the tell-tale signs of growing old which emerge on hands and faces, and to help protect the face from weathering.

It is possible to make one all-purpose cider vinegar lotion which can be used for hair and face. As the aroma of vinegar is distinctive, the aim with this mix is to mask it. Take an ounce (25g) of fresh rosemary (half the quantity if dried) and put it into a saucepan with half a pint (275ml) of water. Bring to the boil and simmer for ten minutes, strain and mix the liquid with half a pint (275ml) of cider vinegar. Further scent it with Eau de Cologne if preferred.

Condition by rubbing a little of the lotion through hair with your hands. Use a tablespoonful after the shampooing process, in the final rinse. It is also possible to use the lotion on the skin as a toner and to bring down muscular swellings.

The consumption of cider vinegar on a regular basis has also been credited with banishing unsightly white spots in fingernails. The spots are a sign of lack of calcium. While vinegar contains only a negligible amount it helps the body make better use of the calcium it takes in.

Household Uses

In the home vinegar is considered a champion of the 'green' trend for its cleaning abilities, none of which threaten the environment. It is a disinfectant, stain remover, floor shiner, metal cleaner and furniture polish. Vinegar is the natural answer to getting whites white in the wash and tackling odours around the house. So versatile is vinegar that it even dispenses with the urban curse of chewing gum stuck to clothes and shoes.

One of the most exciting alternative uses of vinegar is in the making of paper. It is a technique well-known to previous generations but one which has fallen by the wayside in recent years.

Today the most commonly used paper is made from the cell wall of a plant, usually from trees but sometimes from the cotton crop. The vinegar mother is actually cellulose, ready for processing in much the same way as tree pulp. As Lawrence Diggs explains: 'The invisible bacteria are live and they excrete from their bodies something called microbial cellulose which is what you know as paper.'

The mass of mother which appears during brewing and vinegar making is entirely natural. Still makers are compelled to spend time and money disposing of it for the benefit of their end product. It could be turned into a paper with uses as diverse as making rocket casings or as dressings for burn victims.

In this age of conservation, why hasn't cellulose like this taken the paper industry by storm? Lawrence Diggs explains the problems of making paper from animal life rather than plants. In essence the quality of the product reflects the performance of the bacteria, he says:

'This stuff has higher strength to weight ratio than the material they make bullet proof vests from. It comes in different forms, from hard cardboard to tissue paper. But it depends on how the bacteria feel that day.

It is impossible to make a consistent product.' Vinegar paper has been around since people began making vinegar. During World War II and at other times of privation it was used to make shoes in the absence of leather. It can be used as an art medium or even to grow mushrooms in.

Vinegar has long been used in warm water to bring out the colours in worn carpets. Chrome taps marked with water deposits can be made to shine again with a mixture of salt and vinegar or even vinegar and whitening.

It will remove the scale from the inside of a kettle. Half fill the kettle with equal amounts of vinegar and water and boil. Pour the solution away when it has cooled. If the scale is heavily crusted the insides may need a brush. Boiling up vinegar and water in pans will also help eradicate unpleasant cooking odours.

Tarnished brass and copper will be transformed with the cleaning power of hot vinegar and salt. But be sure to rinse the solution off thoroughly afterwards or the cleaner will itself leave marks. Restrict use to door handles and window furniture and use tailor-made modern polishes for items of value. The cleaning power of vinegar can also be put to good use on stained glass, including vases and decanters. Use vinegar in warm water to wash down sealed leather chairs before applying a wax polish. Vinegar has long been recommended in place of bleach for cleaning around the house.

VINEGAR CAN BE EMPLOYED FOR A RANGE OF HOUSEHOLD USES.

Oils and Vinegars Together

Salad dressing

Just a drop or two of balsamic vinegar in olive oil makes a fine salad dressing.

Mayonnaise

Not everyone is convinced of the merits of using olive oil in mayonnaise. The alternatives are sunflower oil or groundnut oil.

Using a mayonnaise base you can produce tartare sauce, usually served with fried fish. Simply take 205 ml or nine fl oz of your homemade mayonnaise and add a finely chopped onion, two chopped boiled eggs, several chopped gherkins and capers to instill that tangy taste and a couple of tablespoons of chopped parsley. Let the mixture stand for an hour before serving.

Marinades

A marinade is a flavoured liquid in which food is drenched or steeped before cooking. Marinades have several purposes. Throughout history they have been used as a short-term preservative and to help tenderise meat, particularly red meat or game. In these days of culinary sophistication a marinade can, with subtle seasoning, enhance a dull joint of meat and transform it into a feast of flavours. With marinades food not only looks more appetising but smells enticingly aromatic too. The marinade also keeps food moist during cooking.

As vinegar has the qualities of a tenderiser it is frequently a staple ingredient of marinades. Oil will prevent food from drying during cooking so it too has a pivotal role, especially in grilling. A pungent, fruity olive oil goes well with red meat or Mediterranean-

style vegetables while Chinese-style food benefits from sesame oil marinades, with the addition of soy sauce, ginger, spices and perhaps chillies. Peanut oil is frequently the preferred choice for white fish and other seafood.

Marinades are either raw or cooked. Raw marinades are most suitable for short use while cooked marinades can successfully preserve meat for several days.

Fruits and sweet foods can also be left in liquids or juices, to achieve similar ends. The process is known as macerating rather than marinading.

OILS AND VINEGARS CAN BE USED TOGETHER IN MAKING CHUTNIES.

GLOSSARY

Acetobactor: Machinery to acidify vinegar.

Mother: Bacterial mass which forms when vinegar is made and during brewing.

Cholesterol: A white, odourless, tasteless globular substance produced in the liver and intestinal tract. It is also found in animal fats. Some cholesterol is vital as it makes and repairs cell membranes among other things and without any we would perish. However, too much is dangerous as it impairs the circulation of the blood.

Free Radicals: Chemicals formed in the body to fight bacteria. When production escalates unchecked – which can happen during illness and exposure to pollution or cigarette smoke – they pose the threat of heart disease and cancer.

Antioxidants: High levels of antioxidant vitamins and minerals are thought to eliminate the conditions which encourage the growth of free radicals.

Low Density Lipoproteins: Type of cholesterol which contributes to heart disease.

High Density Lipoproteins: Type of cholesterol which assists in the fight against heart disease.

Pomace: Low grade olive oil.

Labna: Yoghurt cheese preserved in oil, common in the Middle East.

Pesto: Basil, garlic, pine nut, parmesan and olive oil sauce popular in Italy.

Tannin: Astringent substance derived from oak bark. Present in vinegar following fermentation.

Malting: Process in which barley or another grain is soaked in water, sprouted then kiln-dried.

Cellulose: Carbohydrate which forms the main part of plant cell walls.

Marinate: The process of soaking savoury foods in liquid to preserve them or improve their flavour.

Macerate: The process of soaking fruits in liquids or juices.

INDEX